A Man's Tools For Addressing Betrayal

Keys To Unlocking Freedom & Moving Forward

Sibylle Georgianna, Ph.D.

ISBN 978-1-63877-813-4

Preface

As the one affected by a highly problematic behavior of a person significant to you, each chapter outlines tools and options for you. Use the chapters like you would use an engine-repair manual.

Definitions:

Betrayed Partner

The person who did not step outside the relationship for personal, romantic, sexual or other fulfillment. Other descriptors used are the wounded partner, the betrayed, the injured, the offended party. Note that this does not make the betrayed partner an angel, 100% good, or without areas of improvement.

Unfaithful Party

The person who stepped outside the relationship for personal, romantic, sexual or other fulfillment. Also referred to as the betraying party, the betraying individual, the betrayer. Note that this does not make the betrayer evil, the bad one, the one who always is at fault.

Betrayal

Betrayal, affairs, sex addiction, trauma, and compulsivity impact people of all races, sexual orientation, nationalities, religions, creeds, ethnicities, gender expressions, ages, physical attributes, or mental abilities.

Betrayal can happen through physical, emotional, mental, and/or romantic behaviors. Other ways of betrayal are unfaithfulness by lying, viewing pornography, one-night stands to name a few.

Stigma, shame, and the complexity of situation we find ourselves in can complicate healing and repair and require insights beyond the scope of a book. A list of resources to find trained professionals and educated support groups can be found at the end of this book.

Table of Contents

Preface i

Chapter I: What Just Happened? Discovering An Affair and Betrayal 1

    Some Immediate Options For When You Discover Betrayal: 2

Chapter II: What are you dealing with? Understanding your stress response (it is real) ... 6

    Thirteen Types of Betrayal trauma 7

    There are five types of symptoms that you may feel in response to such an event: 16

Chapter III: All About Triggers 20

Chapter IV: Get Unstuck- Answers to Your Questions 27

    Q&A: What To Expect When Facing Betrayal Trauma 27

Chapter V: Six Questions to Find a Skilled Therapist 34

Chapter VI. What You Can Request: Setting Boundaries 46

Chapter VII: How to Get Your Boundaries Communicated: 55

    Best Practices for Presenting a Request 55

    Successful Behaviors Self-leadership: How to Respond Assertively and Empathetically: 57

Postface 60

Bibliography 65

Copyright © Sibylle Georgianna

Chapter I: What Just Happened? Discovering An Affair and Betrayal

Emergency First Aid Tool Kit:

- Get an STD test;
- Educate yourself about betrayal trauma;
- Get professional support to learn how to interrupt and manage triggers;
- Get support outside of your family and friends until you have decided what educated actions to take, e.g., call into a COSA recovery support meeting and listen (12 step recovery groups do not require you to share);
- You can't "unring a bell". Be careful as to what you share with others about your partner's betrayal.

You may feel that the floor dropped out of your house. A feeling like you are trapped between two trucks on the freeway that are both moving into your lane (with you in between) at the same time. You may experience that things are surreal, as if you are floating and looking at yourself from above.

"I can't stop thinking about it", said Ben as he sat across from me, with a sleep deprived look on his face. He had just found out about his girlfriend's sexually suggestive chatting with another male. He would find out after our time that there was -unfortunately- more than chatting. "Why did I not see this coming? What's wrong with me? Am I not good enough?"

Discovering your significant other's problematic behavior such as cheating, lying can give you an initial feeling of being shell shocked by this type of betrayal. Numb. Powerless.

You, however, have many options available to you. Here are three of them:

Some Immediate Options For When You Discover Betrayal:

(1) Leave the relationship right there and then.

This is most likely the worst option. You may feel that leaving is the only way to recover from this trauma. Leaving without seeing the unfaithful party taking responsibility for his or her actions may create in you, the one leaving, an incomplete grief and unprocessed trauma and betrayal response.

While understandably the responsibility for this breakup is based on your significant other's actions, the breakup may not be one that you chose based on your value system. Thus, you may end up with an undeserved inner conflict and turmoil that, as research shows, does not settle as you leave a relationship.

To the contrary, unresolved emotions may carry over into the next relationship, making it more likely for you to miss warning signs, red flags, and have you end up with strong emotional reactivity (emotions that feel out of control to you or your new significant other).

Not to minimize your pain or to stir up schadenfreude: 90% of affairs (which includes your significant other's behaviors) were found to not lead to a successful relationship. Only 3% of relationships that begin as affairs turn into long-term, sustainable (and cheat-free) marriages .

(2) Stay with the offending party who makes no effort to save your relationship.

When you find yourself with an inactive offending party, you receive the message: "You are not worth my effort." Or "I said I was sorry." Or "Why can't you get over it: I stopped the affair." Or "What else do you want me to do?"

Remedy:

See yourself as worth of the effort of the offending party's repair. That is, you can request from them to get active and into "save the relationship" mode. Otherwise, the inactive party (with their inaction) makes it likely for the relationship to not survive their infidelity.

(3) Watch the offending party's heart-felt, educated effort to repair your relationship and make a value-driven, evidence based decision in the near future

You can predict the success of the offending party's efforts as follows:

The more seriously the one who needs to repair leans into his/her own work (and, with the complexity of your situation, this is best done with a betrayal-trauma trained professional), the higher the chances of success.

For example, you know that your significant other mostly relies on her-/himself but now goes to recovery-focused therapy weekly. In the past, your significant other avoided conversations about hard subjects but is now answering your (understankable) questions.

In the past, your requests triggered your partner's defensiveness and resentment. Now, you see more responsiveness to your requests (even if there is still resentment on the other side). You see the offending partner join you at your counselor's office (which you may have requested many times before but it did not happen until now).

This effort-to-repair attitude in your significant other does not need to mean that you need to reconcile with the offending party. It only means that there was a concerted effort made to undo the damage, learn what is to be learned, and decrease the fallout and long-term negative consequences.

And that you get to decide at some point if the effort made demonstrates to you insight, empathy, and a reason for you to re-invest yourself. Take at least 4-6 months during which you watch the recovery efforts of the other side.

During that time of observation, take good care of yourself: work out, rest well, eat well, get adequate support. Following that observation, you may decide according to your values if you would like to stay or go.

Chapter II: What are you dealing with? Understanding your stress response (it is real)

What you are Dealing With: Betrayal Trauma

Another person's actions have ruptured your relationship with the person who caused the betrayal. This is not your fault. The rupture causes your unfathomable pain. You are hemorrhaging, in need of emergency surgery to stop the bleeding. The one who caused your pain can only imagine how that could feel.

You are not to blame for the betrayal you experienced. It is not your fault. You are not to blame that you are wounded by betrayal; betrayal automatically leaves you feeling as if there is something wrong with you: you were not enough, you were not sexy enough, not romantic enough, you did not talk to your significant other enough. You could have prevented this from happening.

What Is Real?

Your greatest wounding is to believe that nothing that you experienced with your significant other was real. You are experiencing an out-of-the-blue grief response to the sudden loss of what you thought was your life. At some point you need to mourn the relationship you thought you had. Reactions such as anger, sadness, numbness or craving to go out and cheat yourself show the humongous loss. The betrayal wound causes you to no longer trust your significant other and yourself.

You have many questions: Was my relationship with the one who betrayed me an illusion? What's my sense of reality that I did not see the dual life of the one who betrayed me sooner?

How could I have entrusted myself and my family to a person I did not know? You have been wounded on so many levels. I would like to repeat: betrayal trauma is not your fault.

Thirteen Types of Betrayal trauma

Dr. Omar Minwalla identified 13 types of Sex Addiction-Induced Trauma (SAIT) among Intimate Partners and Spouses Impacted by Sex Addiction-Compulsivity©. Note that this does not mean that the one who wounded you is a sex addict. Sex addiction is a clinical diagnosis that needs to be established by a trained professional. At the same time, you may have experienced trauma as found in partners of sex addicts:

1. Discovery Trauma
2. Disclosure Trauma
3. Losing Your Sense of Self
4. Physical Trauma
5. External Crisis

6. Hypervigilance and Re-Experiencing
7. Dynamics of Perpetration, Violation and Abuse (SAIP)
8. Sexual Trauma
9. Gender Wounds and Gender-Based Trauma (GBT)
10. Relational Trauma and Attachment Injuries
11. Family, Communal and Social Injuries
12. Treatment-Induced Trauma
13. Existential and Spiritual Trauma

1. Discovery Trauma:

The discovery of your significant others' behaviors is a critical traumatic incident or event as well as an ongoing traumatic process and system. The impact of a discovery can cause you to feel shattered in your sense of self, a loss of knowing what's reality and what's not, and fear inducing "flight", "freeze", or "flee" mechanisms for human survival.

The discovery is so wounding because your reality is so incongruent with what you thought reality was. Not being able to verify what was deceptive and what not and to assess the extent or nature of the betrayal can cause severe panic, terror, and intense fear, horror, or helplessness.

You may experience multiple and various forms of discovery trauma incidents and processes, sometimes hundreds. Traumatic incidents that repeat many times and have a similar theme can create complex Post Traumtic Stress Disorder (C-PTSD).

Find a trained professional who can support you with processing the traumatic discovery related memories and who can help you establish relational safety.

2. Disclosure Trauma:

Disclosure trauma is a specific type of traumatic discovery incident and traumatic process, and may also occur many times in a partner's experience. Each disclosure is a critical trauma-inducing incident and traumatic process. A disclosure is the process of being told about some aspect of the deceptive, compartmentalized behavior (factual or not).

3. Reality-Ego Fragmentation:

Your sense of reality becomes traumatized and feels shattered. A traumatized, fragmented, and injured sense of reality and yourself causes functional impairment, similar to brain injury.

Changes in your self-perception includes symptom clusters around a sense of helplessness or paralysis of initiative; shame, guilt and self-blame; sense of defilement or stigma; sense of complete difference from others – utter aloneness, sense no one could understand, and a sense of a nonhuman identity (Herman, 1997).

The survival coping reactions to the original impact/trauma creates a new set of feelings, reactions and way one relates to self and others. This is "like waking up one day and you are a different person" and this "sudden different identity" becomes additional trauma, heaped up in addition to the original betrayal trauma (Jason, 2009).

The sudden loss of "self" and "becoming someone different" is also traumatic for children within the parent-child bond/attachment and dependency, causing disturbances and sudden shifts in children, family members, and any human being related intimately or in dependence to you.

4. Impact to Body and Medical Intersection (Dimension 4):

The betrayal can significantly impact your physical body. You can find yourself struggling with how your body looks, find yourself with weight loss or weight gain, vomiting, shaking, hair loss (sometimes extreme), issues with digestion, insomnia and sleep disturbance. Feeling as if you are floating, not knowing how you drove home after finding out, physical expressions of rage such as yelling, speeding, destroying items. You may find yourself scanning your surroundings in hyper-vigilance, with muscle constrictions, aversion to physical or sexual touch to name a few. These are physical and medical symptoms of trauma.

This may be the last thing on your mind, however, taking care of your body is critical. Go for sexually transmitted disease and infections testing as soon as possible. Find a sensitive provider to reduce potential treatment harm based on a provider's insensitivity - if the physician is untrained in betrayal trauma.

5. Trauma due to External Crisis and Destabilization:

An external crisis is due to the sudden or long-term external changes, and the overwhelming chaos that often unfolds as a direct result of the betrayal.

These dynamics are a significant source of stress that alone often can cause you to feel overwhelmed. For instance, having to allocate finances to get treatment for yourself (and possibly your significant other). Coming up with separate sleeping/living arrangements. Changes to routines such as child care, child rearing, deciding on what to say to whom and how to explain the changes that may be noticeable take from your energy and resources.

Often, the person with the affair or "problem behaviors" gets treated as the "identified patient", while you, "the partner" may be expected to "hold down the fort" and "keeping life going" for your and the family. This may result that your trauma gets pushed down and away while you are in "survival" mode. With that, your emotional load increases and may trigger or make worse your trauma load.

6. SAIT Hypervigilance and Re-Experiencing:

According to The Diagnostic and Statistical Manual of Mental Disorders, (Version 5), PTSD is often characterized by heightened sensitivity to potential threats, including those that are related to the traumatic experience (American Psychiatric Association, 2013). The DSM-V describes the symptom of re-experiencing as:

-Intruding spontaneous memories of the traumatic event,

-Recurrent dreams related to it,

-Flashbacks or other intense or prolonged psychological distress.

Symptoms of arousal include:

- "Fight and flight" behaviors,
- Aggression;
- Recklessness or self-destructive behaviors,
- Sleep disturbances,
- Hypervigilance or related problems.

Hyper-arousal and re-experiencing the traumatic experience takes place when specific internal/external "triggers" remind you of the trauma. You react with fear, panic and feelings associated with traumatic memory. Such triggers can feel crippling due to their intensity, frequency and how you find yourself reacting.

Understand your reactions as your body's way to create safety after this immense trauma. You are not "pain shopping", "policing", "playing the victim" Visit Chapter 3 for more information on triggers.

7. Sex Addiction-Induced Perpetration (SAIP):

Psychological and emotional abuse can impact a human being just as much as physical abuse, in terms of harm, symptoms, and traumatic impacts. Emotional abuse includes "gaslighting".

Gaslighting is the process in which the addict intentionally manipulates your reality to keep you from discovery. Gaslighting is a form of psychological manipulation and covert psycho-emotional abuse and perpetration.

While your gut may have told you that something was not quite right, gaslighting causes you to set aside your gut feelings. You stopped listening to your gut. However, your connection between your mind and your intuitive gut feeling is a fundamental survival mechanism. You may find yourself confused, lost, and unable to stand up for yourself.

8. Sexual Trauma:

Betrayal trauma can affect your sexuality. Sex may be the last thing on your mind or the first and foremost thing (post-trauma-induced-hypersexuality). You desire numbing or zoning out, escaping from fear and panic about having contracted a disease or infection of a sexually transmitted disease. Flashbacks about specific acts that the betrayer engaged in can intrude your awareness out of the blue. You may feel yourself avoiding touch and physical contact.

You may deeply question your role as a father and male. You get mad at yourself for desiring sex with the person who betrayed you.

9. Gender Related Trauma:

You, a male partner, can find yourself profoundly impacted at the core of your gender and gender identity: what you think of yourself as as a husband, father, man, human being, etc.

You may be blamed or blame yourself as a victim. As hard as it may be to believe: you are not to blame for significant's acting out behaviors.

10. Relational Trauma and Attachment Injuries:

Relational trauma and attachment injuries due to betrayal have ruptured your coupleship or relationships. The relationship, the "us" itself, is traumatized. You may find yourself reacting in ways you never imagined. Your relational trauma trauma is so great that your coping has been compromised

11. Family, Communal and Social Trauma:

Your trauma can also overshadow your other relationships, including how you relate to your children, your extended family, and others while being in public or within your usual social circles. It is important to acknowledge that this social impact of the trauma may involve multiple attachment injuries, significant grief and loss with regards to other relationships.

12. Treatment-Induced Trauma:

Treatment-induced trauma is a clinical or medical intervention that causes you harm instead of healing. Therapists and/or medical professionals "re-injure" you instead of facilitating your post-traumatic healing and growth.

This may stem from a provider's lack of proper education about betrayal trauma. A provider who has a traditional "co- addiction model" for treatment views you, the partner of someone with a highly problematic behavior/addiction as someone with an "addiction", not as someone who needs treatment for complex post traumatic stress. Others may view you as "codependent" or as someone who needs to learn better communication and anger management skills. "Sex positive" counselors and educators will prescribe, "date nights or sex night" to "reconnect" after betrayal.

Treatment providers who mislabel well-established trauma symptoms (both PTSD and CPTSD) in such ways create damage and trauma to you, the betrayer, your coupleship. and family.

13. Spiritual and Existential Trauma:

Your faith and how you relate to God can be severely traumatized. You cannot imagine how a loving God can allow for betrayal to happen. You may find your faith shattered deep within your soul.

Betrayal Trauma Hijacks Your Brain's Stress Response

Research shows that people who discover affairs and betrayal can experience a stress response. Note that a trained professional is needed to establish a diagnosis. Signs of a so called acute stress reaction follow:

You were exposed to a stressful situation where you

1. Directly experienced the traumatic event(s) or
2. Witnessed, in person, the event(s) as it occurred to others or
3. Learned that the event(s) occurred to someone close to you or
4. Experienced repeated exposure to aversive details.

There are five types of symptoms that you may feel in response to such an event:

1. "Intrusion" Symptoms

- You may find yourself with recurrent, involuntary, and intrusive memories that strongly distress you. This can include recurrent distressing thoughts about the discovery, dreams, flashbacks that make you feel or acts as if the traumatic event(s) was happening *right now*. This memories can be "triggered" (see below) in such intensity that you lose track of your present surroundings. Instead of checking your grocery list in the store, you may find yourself driving home, needing to check the phone bill.

- Cues that symbolize or resemble an aspect of the traumatic event(s) trigger intense or prolonged psychological distress. For example, your significant other's affair partner drove a red sports car. You find yourself sweating and with intense anger after seeing a red sports car while you are on the way to the car wash.

2. Negative Mood

- You may feel as if you completely lost your ability to experience positive emotions. For example, you find yourself numb in response to your children (towards whom you had strong loving feelings prior to the betrayal). People may look and you and ask you "What happened to your sense of humor?" You feel that, e.g., your zest for life, your sense of humor, and your spontaneity are completely wiped out. Read more below to find out how to get yourself back.

3. "Dissociative" Symptoms (AKA Disconnected Memories)

- An altered sense of the reality of your surroundings or yourself (e.g., seeing yourself from another's perspective, being in a daze, time slowing)
- Inability to remember an important aspect of the traumatic event(s) (typically due to dissociative amnesia and not to other factors such as head injury, alcohol, or drugs).

4. Avoidance Symptoms

- Although you are usually a go-getter, you find yourself hibernating at home. Despite of a full calendar, you find yourself numbing or spacing out (e.g., drinking, video games, binge watching Netflix). This happens so that you can avoid the extremely distressing memories, thoughts, or feelings about the discovery and event(s) of betrayal.
- You find yourself avoiding reminders of what happened (e.g., people, places, conversations, activities, objects, situations). You find yourself forgetting about meeting joint friends. You are driving a different way to pick up the kids from school.

5. "Arousal" Symptoms (AKA Your Nervous System Is Running on Overdrive)

- Sleep disturbance (e.g., difficulty falling or staying asleep, restless sleep).
- Irritable behavior and angry outbursts (with little or no provocation). You are known for your negotiating skills but find yourself throwing dishes and speeding on the freeway.
- Hypervigilance. You feel that the shoe is dropping at any time. Your mind keeps going "There must be more." You are always watchful and cannot seem to settle down. One answer by the offending party leads to your next question.
- Problems with concentration.

- Exaggerated startle response: You find yourself jumping when someone pulls up behind you at the gas station to get gas. Your heart starts racing, you start sweating and are reminded of when you were deployed.

A professional can help you identify if the above symptoms can be part of a so called "acute stress response" or of Post Traumatic Stress. Also, ask the professional to give you tools to de-activate reactivity and the aforementioned "triggers" of your stress response.

Chapter III: All About Triggers

There are two types of trigger:

(1) Internal triggers

Internal triggers involve some type of emotional discomfort: depression, shame, anxiety, anger, fear, guilt, remorse to name a few. For example, the person with the problematic behaviors is at work and you feel you are losing your sanity. This emotional discomfort may trigger a desire to check all credit card records and bank statements, drive by his/her work and checking if the car is there.

(2) External triggers

External triggers are people, places, things (including emojis) and/or events. For example, you learn that the person with the problematic behaviors texted with an affair partner when you were in the same room.

Triggers can be interwoven (e.g., be both internal and external). For example, you argue with your significant other to get more information on what happened (an external trigger), you will likely experience emotional discomfort (e.g., disgust, anxiety, depression: internal triggers), which both may trigger insecurity and your desire to get more information

The daunting news is that almost anything can be a trigger. The good news in this situation is that trigger management is a learned skill. You can manage and gently deactivate triggers by (1) Identifying them, (2) Breathing and (3), choosing an alternative action to take.

The goal of your work is not that there are no more triggers coming your way, but that you will be able to identify them and keep on your course of action instead of getting side tracked. The good news is also that trigger management will also help you in other parts of life that are challenging (e.g., difficult situations on the job or with family members).

Trigger Protocol:

(1) Identifying the trigger.

This might be hard at first as triggers seem to come out of nowhere. You may find yourself caught in a stress response that gets you from 0 to 100 in less than 2 seconds. To list a couple of situation where your stress understandably gets triggered:

- You find yourself getting angry while driving to the store;
- You look at a family photo and realize that the affair was already going on during the time when the picture was taken;
- Your significant other is getting a phone call from an unknown phone number and shows her phone to you as it rings.

Seeing yourself upset means that you were triggered. You will *not* need to know the exact trigger and why the emotions you are experiencing got triggered. Simply state to yourself "Am I triggered?", "I see I'm triggered", "It feels silly but I am triggered."

Think about this as if you would walk over to your friend in the gym who seems upset. You would ask him if he is ok. Use that same attitude towards yourself when you are triggered.

(2) Breathing.

Breathing orients you to the here and now. In the present moment, remind yourself that you are safe now. Nothing bad is happening now, right in this moment. Yes, the betrayal happened and are feeling upset in this moment. Is the person acting out right this second? If you are triggered, your body is telling you that the betrayal is happening right now, when it happened in the past.

A note: If your significant other is still entangled in the affair, your gut will give you continued alarm signals until the affair partner stops her behavior. To get your gut calmed down (and you with the continuous feeling that indeed, the affair is over), a therapeutic intervention is the preferred way to proceed.

The therapeutic invention that research studies found essential for healing from betrayal within a relationship is a so called formal disclosure. A formal disclosure is facilitated by a therapist who is trained in betrayal trauma and addiction recovery. The betraying individual sits down with you in the therapist office and walks you through the parameters of the problematic behaviors. Frequency of behaviors. Money spent. Other people affected. No gory details (details do not help you heal but give you additional triggers that we would want to keep out of your live) but enough information so that you know what you are dealing with. Often a disclosure is accompanied by a polygraph- physiological evidence of the betraying individual's answers as being truthful.

(3) Choosing an alternative action to take.

You *can* request your partner to support you and work through the triggers together. What is an alternative action to engage in? If that's hard to know, seek support from a sex&love addiction/betrayal trauma specialist to guide you. Alternative actions include:

Bilateral Body Movements:

Move your body's left and right sides in an alternating fashion, e.g., tap your right and then your left foot, right, left, right left,... (50 repetitions). Tap your collar bone left, right, left, right, etc.. Other examples of that movement: boxing, riding a bike, paddling out to surf, running, walking.

If you are not able to move (e.g., you are at work), you can set up bilateral movement of your body by listening to sounds that are sent to your headphones in an alternating fashion. Look up and listen to Youtube "EMDR Bilateral Stimulation Music" (see above). Listen to that music using your phone's headset- the rhythm sent to your ears in an alternating fashion will calm down your brain.

Longer: 60 min version.

Shorter: 37 min version.

Light exercise (most often that includes bilateral movement as described above):

Take a brief walk; run a flight of stairs, lifting some weights (heavy items at work/home qualify).

Communication

-Take breaks from talking about this difficult topic (especially early in the morning and after 8 p.m. at night);

-As much as it is in your control, choose the time for communication with others about emotionally difficult subjects as conducive to your schedule and energy levels. If you are the one needing to propose a different time for the conversation, promptly let the person know which time will work for you (and then take the lead to initiate the conversation during the time you proposed)

-Consider a support group for talking (not just with friends or family members0). "Outsourcing" such a difficult topic to a setting where others (in the support group) understand and can get with where you are at allows your friendships to be unaffected by the heavy topic of betrayal.

Talk to (and possibly share) people who are sensitive to your current needs. If you are dealing with an addiction (or an addiction in a loved one), consider a 12 step community for education and support. E.g. 24 hours online support: https://www.intherooms.com/ or look up an in-person 12 step meeting by googling "12 Step meeting locator".

Resting/Sleep

-If you cannot fall asleep, see your time as time of resting instead. Resting helps your body relax and replenish.

Thought and Emotion Stopping Strategies

"The Three Second Rule"

-Second 1: I feel *something* / have recurring thoughts that I cannot slow down

-Second 2: Interrupt and ask yourself: What is my strategy?

-Second 3: Pick and apply one of the above strategies

"Bathroom Break"

Step away from what you are doing by going to the bathroom (or another place with running water) to wash your hands. This will move your body's sensations to a more calm state.

"Ice Cube Break"

Step away from what you are doing by getting some ice (e.g., vending machine, ice cube tray) and hold the ice in your hands. Notice the cool sensation. The cool sensation can help you gently shift your behavior and/or feelings.

"Unfreeze/Thawing Down"

Our mind/emotions/body can feel like going into the aforementioned "freeze" or "collapse" if we experience a longer period of stress. If you feel you are slowed down (e.g., feel your brain is foggy, feel you cannot move, feel too heavy to get out of bed), seek some (therapeutic) support to gently release the stress response of your body. All of the above strategies can help you to move from feeling stuck or "frozen" to unstuck.

Chapter IV: Get Unstuck- Answers to Your Questions

Q&A: What To Expect When Facing Betrayal Trauma

Research shows that the brain is affected by acute stress and trauma. The trauma from betrayal is so great that your prefrontal cortex (the part of the brain that guides your decision making, problem solving, and other sophisticated ways of thinking) goes offline. It is easy to get impatient when the brain is affected. What to expect:

Q: Every time I share about the betrayal I start feeling so overwhelmed I am shutting down. That is a turnoff for most people (including for me). What do I do?

A: Byron Katie calls an attachment to a deeply embedded belief the reason for suffering. Current research on partners of unfaithful significant others shows an acute stress response (often post-traumatic stress) as the reason for suffering. When you are in a state of chronic post-traumatic stress, your body's stress response is focused on your survival, Your ability to make complex decisions is impaired.

You may feel your survival response as fight or flight, frozen, or both. Your body's stress response wants to keep you in the replay of the discovery, the re-experiencing of the worst moment, just to make sure that you are doing everything that you can to keep yourself alive. Using one or several of the aforementioned alternative actions allows your body to move out that understandable stress response.

Q: What if I encounter the same triggers over and over again? Does it mean that I am not healing?

A: Understandably you may ask how many more times you need to breathe, count what your senses tell you, or lift weights to get the anger out. What matters is that every time you are using a healthy stress-reduction strategy, you are guiding your body to not attach to the nightmare. You are not to blame for the betrayal. It is not your fault that you are triggered. Use strategies to interrupt the triggers.

Instead, you get to have healthy control over what you -realistically- can control: your responses in the here-and-now. While you would like to move forward (and rest assured, I am putting this book together because I desire for you to move forward), we also want to give you the time you need to sort through what happened. At some point, it will be the right time to grieve your losses.

I am not saying that you won't get a chance to work on each trigger: You get to work on that when you choose to, perhaps with the help of a skilled therapist who specializes in trauma treatment. The strategies found in this book tell you what to do in the in-between times and when your brain is getting hijacked by a trigger.

In other words: You get to move as quickly as you like and as fast as your body wants to allow it. For example, if you find yourself "forgetting" appointments, erasing your counselor's contact info, it may be that your body is blocking your work. You may find yourself moving two steps forward and one step back.

If you feel a push and pull between your mind who says "go ahead", "move on", or "why are you still looking back?" and your body who seems to forget, "space out" or "not get it", it's time to slow yourself down. You may find yourself getting impatient with your body (which includes your heart). At the same time, when both heart and mind have the option to be at peace with one another, you will notice that you are moving forward.

An example: Your significant other wants to reconcile with you. She found out that her (maladaptive) behaviors that caused you an avalanche of flashbacks are not worth pursuing, but that you are. You may find yourself in the tension of your mind saying "What are you waiting for? This is what you wanted- her coming back in a contrite fashion, wanting to make the relationship better than ever!"

At the same time, your heart might wonder if you ever going to be able to trust her again? How long it will take to not feel triggered anymore? And if one can truly recover from what happened? And what "returning to normal" is anyway? Take the time to attend to the questions of your heart and to find answers that are within your values. You will notice -with patience and perseverance in self-care and trauma reduction- that the tension between your mind and your heart will lessen.

Q: What can I do if I find myself self-sabotaging my growth instead of pursuing it? Avoiding the pursuit of my health at my own expense?

A: Rest assured that avoiding is a perfectly normal response in the face of this huge stressor. And, by reading this, you are not completely avoiding the resources that are out there for you 9. You get to be gentle with yourself: perhaps the way how you currently are handling your pain may feel like the only way that you can handle the intense feelings.

When you are ready, you will grow sick of the "old" way of handling your pain (e.g., avoiding, numbing). Currently, you may not (yet) really care to get out of your pain. You may not be ready to give up the avoiding, the numbing.

May I suggest -since I hate to see people suffer- that you seek some support. A professional who can help you move past the anxiety and depression that often linger beneath avoidance and numbing. A trained professional can help you with putting into place new ways to relate to yourself (e.g., when you are lonely, anxious, or are feeling low). The counselor can walk you through other options besides avoidance and numbing. You are worth it!

Q.: I cannot get a commitment from my partner- she says that she is not sure about what she can offer in our relationship. This makes me feel even more anxious and overwhelmed.

A. While it may feel that you have so much to deal with, the betraying partner has equally (if not more) to work on. Affairs stem from an attachment failure of the betraying party: instead of coming to you for comfort, attention, and support, she chose the affair as a coping mechanism.

If the affair was driven by an addiction behavior (which is what a certified sex addiction therapist can help your significant other with), it may take 3-5 years for her brain to heal from their addictive behaviors and create new brain pathways for healthy attachment to be built.

Q: I have been working on forgiving my significant other for her/his infidelity for a long time, but whoever I consult with seems to give me the same advice: to stay put, to not let my guard down. How can I forgive?

Every situation is complex, intricate, and needs to be handled with customized care and caution. It is quite common that the one searching for a solution and potentially the one(s) who want to provide a solution operate with a -known or unknown- motive.

What's wrong with having a motive, you ask? Well, it depends on your motive- are you, the one seeking healing, convinced that your significant other will cheat again? Do the counselor(s) you inquire with have a motive? Do they want you to know *your* truth? Are the one(s) you consult with wanting to prove you that the answer they give is valid?

In *The Grief Recovery Handbook* (written by John James and Russell Friedman), the authors state that your declaration "I decide to not let the past hurt me anymore."

is your declaration of forgiveness. The authors described their successful work with many who went through loss and betrayal: A series of small and correct action choices will get you past the losses that your situation created, bring breakthrough on the important subject of forgiveness, and complete the difficult emotions that come with the complex situation you are dealing with.

Q: What about my partner? What can I request from her?

It may take time for you to heal. You can speed up your recovery by seeking support by a professional who can guide you with "somatic" focused treatment to reduce the post-traumatic stress response. The same is true for the offending party's stress response: we would want both the betrayer and the betrayed to heal from betrayal and pain as quickly as possible.

Often, problematic behaviors are driven by former traumatic experiences. When it comes to recovering from traumatic experiences, the aforementioned techniques to resolve trauma are equally beneficial (and necessary) for the one with the problematic behaviors. Feel free to share this information with them. At the same time, the most healthy control you have with regards to your own decisions and choices. Focusing on your personal healing in this time will get you the furthest, as it may inspire your partner to do the same.

Q: I have talked to numerous counselors, but none of them could tell me how they could get me out of my pain without signing me up for at least 20 sessions of "my own" therapy (as they put it). What can I request from my counselor?

A: You can be picky as you are interviewing a counselor to support you with meeting your unique needs. If you are finding your answers from "old motives" that have not worked for you before ("therapists are just a bunch of …"), make a written list of how you want this situation turn around for you. Share the turnaround with trustworthy people who do not judge you but who are your biggest fans in this difficult season. This person could be your friend, your empathetic great-aunt, a same-sex coworker who has been through the same thing and who confided in you when he was struggling, or a specialized therapist. With more processing, healing can evolve quicker. No matter what format of support fits for you best, the ingredients of your success are within your control. Attending to your stress response sets free your ability to self-reflect and inquire. This allows you to mourn your losses and to complete/leave behind complex emotional experiences.

Chapter V: Six Questions to Find a Skilled Therapist

Interview Questions to Find a Skilled Therapist

- "Are you a Certified Sex Addiction Therapist (CSAT)?"
- Have you heard of partner trauma? Are you trained in betrayal trauma?
- Are you trained in somatic therapy (e.g., EMDR Therapy, EFT)? How will you help me with triggers?
- How many sessions do you think I need to feel better?
- How will you help me with decreasing sessions when I am at the end of my treatment?

Dr. Robert Scaer is medical expert who spent years as a rehabilitation neurologist.

In his book "8 keys to brain-body balance", he provides an excellent overview as to which parts of the body are actively involved in our stress responses. He also describes that we can use the messages of the body to heal itself from that stress response: what happens in the brain drives how the body reacts.

In therapy, the trained therapist can partner with the client and together teach the client's brain that memories of stressful events can gently be extinguished. Yes, you are reading correctly: your body is able to completely let go of an ingrained stress response!

Dr. Scaer looks at various therapeutic techniques. Those that gently downshift the part of the brain that is turned on when we are stressed during the therapeutic sessions allow the traumatic memory to lose its power, and for difficult feelings and sensations such as fear, shame, freezing, fight or flight to settle. This means that you will still remember difficult situations, yet you don't feel drained or other feelings and sensations that went hand and hand with that traumatic memory. As one client stated after she finished processing heartbreaking neglectful circumstances that she endured during her early childhood years "It was hard, but I made it. I am not defined by it."

Based on Dr. Scaer's research, you can find a fitting therapist by asking them about their tools for helping you downshift your body's stress response in a solution focused way. That type of therapy can be short-term.

With a caring therapist and a calm brain, what your body saved up as a sensation of stress will gently be released if the following 6 things are provided during the therapy sessions: (1) learning to stay in the present moment, (2) a healthy ritual, (3) empowerment, (4) brain activity that activates the left to the right side of the brain in an alternating fashion, (5) a completion of what was felt in the body, and (6) repair of perceptions.

Ask the therapist who states that they are somatically trained to tell you *how* they specifically will work you with reduce your trauma. With betrayal trauma, clients often feel powerless and helpless. Interviewing a therapist that is supposed to help you gain clarity and move past betrayal and pain is an active approach to move forward. Choosing a therapist deliberately will empower you to remain in charge even if your sense of healthy power has taken a hit from the betrayal trauma. You can ask your therapist the following questions:

(1) How will you teach me to stay in the present moment?

For example, learning to take a deep breath, pray, or visualization can be calming. A skilled therapist can help you with staying grounded.

(2) What healthy rituals are you using during therapy? Which healthy rituals can help me outside of therapy?

Healthy rituals inhibit the emotional part of the brain that runs our stress responses. Healthy rituals counteract intrusive thoughts, calm down ruminations and obsessions, and move your body and mind back into balance, which, in term, help your healing.

Rituals can be simple. For my clients, I end our time by record a thing or two that spoke to them during the therapy sessions. They can listen to the recording outside of their sessions. Other rituals include guiding clients through a brief meditation at the end of the session so that they can leave with calm and peace, even when they worked on an upsetting event during the therapy session.

(3) How are you empowering me during our sessions?

Ideally, if we grew up with a caregiver that was attuned to what we needed and provided in a consistent fashion, it allows us to feel a sense of empowerment later on in life. Often we grow up with imperfect parents and with deficits in empowerment.

It may leave us with a sense that we don't have much to say, we have to make the best of what we are being presented with. We may struggle with turning down opportunities that we do not wish to pursue, or with feeling overcommitted to situations that are not ideal for us.

As the person who you choose to work with how he/she will empower you. Find out how they will help you if they disagree with what you are looking for. For example, you might find yourself wanting 3-5 consultations but they may want you to do more sessions.

You have the right to ask the therapist upfront and then decide *after* the session if the therapist is a good fit. How is the therapist helping his/her clients to finish their treatments? The way how the therapist shares about their way of helping clients wean off their sessions will give you a good idea of how sensitive the therapist is to what you want.

If it feels to overwhelming to think of ending therapy when you are in the process of finding a good therapist, don't worry. At the same time, you deserve to "shop around" for a therapist who is a good fit!

(4) How will you help me with completing what I am dealing with? How will you help me move past what happened?

A trauma trained therapist will help you define healthy boundaries for what you need during this difficult time. In addition to helping you set and maintain such boundaries with the person with the problematic behavior, a somatically trained therapist will help your body to "complete" the body's movement as commonly found with physical stress responses.

As you would hear the cooling device in your car still running after you have turned off your car's engine, think of therapy as a way to cool off and turn of the engine of your stress response. That's what Dr. Scaer found for his patients as well as from his personal life: with a therapist who is trained in understanding and guiding your body, you get take a quick peak at the traumatic memory (that's all that is necessary) and then allow your body to complete and release the stress response that was stored with the traumatic memory.

Sounds scary? Think about it like this: when we are stressed (for example, when we are dealing with a traumatic situation), your body goes into a stress response such as freezing or fight/flight. Your body stores the memory of freeze and fight/flight as a so called "procedural" memory: a memory of a process or movement of your body. Other examples of procedural memories are knowing how to drive a car or bike, how to tie your shoe laces, how to shoot a basketball.

A procedural memory in an overwhelming and/or a traumatic experience can come in two flavors: (1) we experience us as unable to move/say something ("freeze"); (2) we fight back/get angry/attack ("fight/flight"). None of those two procedural memory is better than the other. Sometimes we are more embarrassed about our freeze response than about our fight/flight response. At the same time, both need to be gently attended to so that they stop interfering with our current well-being and peace of mind. You, the client, get to be actively involved in allowing your body to complete that stress response. This type of therapeutic work is called "somatic" work because it helps your body to release the stress response. You get to ask what specific techniques the therapist uses. Examples of such techniques follow.

(5) Are you doing somatic work with your clients?

A therapist with an emphasis of somatic work will, for example, ask you where you are feeling a situation in your body. Finding where you have a "felt sense" of an experience allows your body to gently access that procedural memory that stored the "felt sense" of the trauma. Together with a skillful therapist, you get to finish/complete that stress response, relieving you from pain, shame, and other parts of the stressful situation you encountered.

The therapist can facilitate this by, e.g., talking you through the difficult situation, or guiding you through imagery. Like athletes who get coached through a game that's ahead of them and who get to imagine every move they are making, the therapist will coach you through the difficult situation you have been facing, all the way to finishing the stress response.

What "finishing" a stress response means:

- You set your body and mind free for moving forward and past feeling stuck;
- You teach your body that, while it was horrible to deal with what you have been through, the experience does not have to limit you. Instead, this work is giving you what we call "mental resilience";
- Enhanced ways to deal with future situations may be stressful;
- Better decision making (especially complex decisions often found with betrayal);
- Improved health outcomes (e.g., you may find your blood pressure to become more normal, sleep/rest better, and find yourself overall being more relaxed).

What "finishing" a stress response does not mean:

- You will stop being vigilant or safe.

Instead, the boundaries that you get to set up toward the unfaithful one will provide safety so that your mind and body can settle.

- Saying that what happened wasn't really that bad.

Instead, we acknowledge the stress response that it caused you and allow for the stress response to no longer overshadow how you think or feel.

- Letting the person who betrayed you off the hook.

Instead, you can decide how you would like to proceed with the relationship if the betraying party is not adhering to the boundaries you are requesting. Is it time to put in more distance so that the betraying party can experience how it would feel if you are no longer there for her/him?

- Doubting that the betrayal really happened.

Instead, your work will allow you to refer back to the betrayal whenever you wish, yet you will not have to go there and relive it with full force in a repetitive fashion. A comparison to files on your computer: With allowing your body to process the stress response, it's as if your brain can move the cursor over the file and reference it, yet it does not have to go to a file and open the file again and again. Doing your work here will allow your mind to stop painful and energy absorbing obsessions.

- Forcing you to give up your values and/or identity.

Instead, you can ask your therapist to clarify your values and to make decisions according to what you value.

- You won't get justice.

Instead, resolving your own stress response will empower you to be proactive and efficient in what *you* can do and what you *can* ask for. It will allow you to *not* take on what the betraying party needs to work on: Developing insight in the pain that the betraying party caused you, taking responsibility for the betrayal wounds, and developing empathy towards you.

- You need to be over/done with your suffering.

Instead, as you help your body to release the trauma, it will allow you to regain the clarity about what you value. You can take the time that you deserve. The good news about the release of a stress response is that it can be quickly with a skilled therapist.

Often, the betraying partner's understandable difficulties with seeing you in the excruciating pain of betrayal leads to impatience with *your* recovery. At the same time, we can trust that the betraying party can learn to become patient and supportive of you through these circumstances

- Taking away your sympathizing with other people who are in pain while you get to feel OK.

Rest assured that you will not need to worry about that. Instead, your own work will deepen your empathy (should it need deepening).

- Not caring about the person/thing/value that you lost.

Instead, your work will allow you to care and grief during times that you desire to revisit the pain, and set aside the grief and pain during other times. Your therapeutic work will allow you to care for what you value without having your stress response interfere. That is, you get focus on work, relationships, hobbies as usual, according to what you value.

- I will forget what happened if I'm not in pain.

Understandably, the powerlessness over an unfathomable, traumatic event has prevented the fulfillment of a survival or necessary need in you. Examples of necessary needs are to be asked for permission, to have a choice/other options at hand. Because those survival needs must be filled in some way, the body in the traumatic situation creates the fulfillment by "hooking" your healthy need or desire with the dysfunctional behavior of the other party.

We make excuses for the betraying party. We think their behavior is our fault. We feel guilty to stand up for what we need. You may find yourself returning unconsciously to excusing unhealthy behaviors because it is actually an attempt of your mind to get your needs met. With your own work and getting a resolution from the trauma caused, you are actually *enhancing* the clarity and understanding of what happened, along with greater clarity of what you need

- I will lose my connection to the betraying party if I'm not in pain.

Instead, your own work will allow you to gently create a healthy attachment to the betraying person: (1) if you choose plus (2) *when good boundaries and recovery of the betrayer are put in place.*

Your own stress-reduction therapy creates healthy connection with yourself. This can release you from feeling "hooked up" with your significant other, having to make work whatever the offending party can offer. As you have repaired your connection with yourself and have gained clarity about your boundaries, you also no longer find yourself returning to a person who is not (yet) healthy.

You ask how I would know? According to research, if we find ourselves returning to behaviors and/or relationships not good for us, it points us to an (unconscious) attempt to fulfill the survival or an unfulfilled need that could not (yet) be resolved from earlier trauma. At the same time: you will be able to resolve it now.

(6) How are you working with your clients to restore any impairment of their day-to-day view of life that has been compromised by traumatic memory?

Understandably, if an accident or unforeseen event happens in the space of the client (e.g., in front of their eyes, to their left), the body quickly takes a note. This creates a sensitivity in clients that may impair well-being and undisturbed enjoyment of life.

For example, you find yourself tightening up after a car accident whenever you are driving and you notice that cars around you are slowing down suddenly. Survivor of combat feel panicked in narrow supermarket aisles.

Pay attention if the therapist you are considering is sensitive to also helping you de-stress from perceptions or memories that were shaped by the event(s) that leads you to seeking help. Such memories, if they remain unattended, can create a sense of uncomfortableness or unease. Decreasing such difficult sensations is important, and a sensitive therapist will be able to help you with that.

Other recommendations to speed up your healing process are those that help your body in optimizing its immune function and capacities to regenerate its cells by, e.g.,:

-Avoiding unhealthy foods and limiting alcohol;

-Limiting use of prescription (legal) and illegal drugs/substances;

-Getting as much sleep as possible;

-Working out regularly;

-Using meditation and other ways to activate your body's built-in relaxation response (e.g., martial arts).

No matter what approach you are choosing, rest assured that you have choices, can make requests, and will be able to move forward! While this situation understandably has impacted you, it will not need to define you and your future.

Chapter VI. What You Can Request: Setting Boundaries

Telling the betraying party what you need is the next step in beating betrayal. What do you need to put in place? What needs to be removed? This may feel like a daunting task. Below are examples on what you could request.

Non-negotiable Boundaries

I will not tolerate the following behaviors in our relationship (to be adjusted):

1. Sexual acting out of any type.

2. Repeated lying, gaslighting, vagueness, or deflecting from the truth.

3. Looking at porn/masturbating.

4. Collecting pornographic pictures or pictures of people you're attracted to.

5. Inappropriate ways of interacting with others, e.g., flirting, winking or similar gestures (including interacting online (texting, social media: use of emojis).

6. Reading online and watching shows that degrade, e.g., married men.

8. Going on dating platforms or other similar websites.

9. Messaging someone with the intent of having a sexual encounter or masturbating.

10. Having sexual encounters of any type with another person, or bot.

11. Using sex toys.

12. Going on chat rooms.

13. Contact with any acting out partner or crush.

14. Not deleting and blocking acting out partners and crushes.

15. Not going to regular therapy sessions with a therapist trained in sex and love addiction recovery.

16. Not having accountability software on all devices.

17. Not having GPS tracking on you whenever you're away from home without me.

18. Getting a new or using someone else's computer device/phone without telling me beforehand.

19. Discussing sensitive relationship topics with your family or mine, unless the details are mutually agreed upon (see communication boundaries below).

20. Changing passwords, signing up for new apps/accounts, not telling me about apps/accounts you still have.

21. Not disclosing a slip, trigger or lie within 24hrs of it happening.

22. Not taking a polygraph every 6-12 months.

23. Withholding physical access to your phone, computer, or other devices, notepads, etc.

24. Altering or deleting Internet, phone/text history, contacts or location data, social media friends/chats/messaging.

25. "Switching" your problematic actions to another outlet (e.g., video gaming, binge watching Netflix, self-loathing, rescuing the vulnerable) instead of working on yourself.

26. Refusing to work on yourself (e.g., delaying therapy, half-heartedness in health related commitments).

If these behaviors are violated, I will consider (one or more of the following):

1. Withholding sex with you.
2. Requesting from you that you sleep in the other room (or moving into another room myself).
3. Requesting that you go to more therapy with a specialist.
4. Having us go to more therapy with a specialist.
5. Requesting you take a polygraph within 24 hours of the discovery.
6. Requesting you get a STD test.

7. Temporarily separating while we are working with our therapists on individual health and recovery goals.

8. Request that you move out (or move out myself).

9. Ending the relationship.

Physical Boundaries

At this time, these are the physical boundaries I need to set with you in order to feel safe in our relationship:

1. I will be the one to initiate touch.

2. Let me finish what I am doing (when I'm in the middle of doing something).

3. Keep "big" conversations for after work, no later than 9 p.m.

If these boundaries are violated, I will take the following steps to protect myself (one or more of the following):

1. Ask you to stop.

2. Take space from you.

3. Dress and shower in private.

4. Have you to sleep in the other room.

5. Withhold sex from you.

Sexual Boundaries

At this time, these are the sexual boundaries I need to set with you in order to feel safe in our relationship:

1. I will be the one to initiate sex or sex play.
2. Please refrain from making suggestive comments, grabbing my body parts, joking about sex.

If these boundaries are violated, I will take the following steps to protect myself (one or more of the following):

1. Ask you to stop.
2. Take space from you.
3. Dress and shower in private.
4. Have you to sleep in the other room.
5. Withhold sex from you.

Emotional Boundaries

At this time, these are the Emotional boundaries I need to set with you in order to feel safe in our relationship:

1. I need you to seek support for your addiction from your therapists, accountability partners and work group members and not your family, my family, my friends or me.

2. If I become triggered, I need you to give me space and time to work through it without you getting defensive, mad, minimizing my feelings.

3. I need you to tell me the truth and with the level of detail I'm asking for.

4. Work with your certified sex addiction therapist which actions you can take to make me feel safe.

5. Communicate to me ahead of time how you will be accountable while you're away from home so I know you're not engaging in inappropriate behaviors.

If these boundaries are violated, I will take the following steps to protect myself (chose one or more):

1. Ask you to stop.

2. Take space from you.

3. Ask you to go to more therapy with a specialist.

4. Withhold sex with you.

5. Temporarily separate from you.

6. Have you move out.

7. Have you sleep in the other room.

8. Have you take a polygraph.

9. Have us go to therapy with a specialist together.

10. End the relationship.

Other Boundaries

These are the other boundaries I need to set with you in order to feel safe in our relationship:

1. Block pornography or written erotica from coming into our home by using filtering software and by using the computer and phone in a "public" place of the house (e.g., dining room table, kitchen counter, not in the bathroom).

2. Stop contact with people who have joined in, encouraged, or looked the other way when you engaged in any of the behaviors.

If these boundaries are violated, I will take the following steps to protect myself (choose one or more):

1. Ask you to downgrade your phone (flip phone).
2. Password protect computer access.
3. Take space from you.
4. Ask you to go to more therapy.
5. Have us go to more couple's therapy.
6. Withhold sex with you.
7. Temporarily separate from you.
8. Have you move out.
9. Have you sleep in the other room.
10. Have you take a polygraph.
11. End the relationship.

COMMUNICATION PLAN WITH OTHERS (FAMILY, FRIENDS, CHILDREN, ETC.)

1. What we will tell: Nothing. If they don't already know, they don't need to be told. If they know, we tell them "we are continuing to work on the issue between the two of us and with our therapists".

2. Who we will share this information with: Therapists, 12 step sponsor with solid recovery, work groups and support groups.

3. Who will do the telling: Both of us (individually with therapist, sponsor, 12 step share).

4. When will this information be shared: As needed (e.g., during weekly meetings).

5. All topics are only discussed in the presence of a therapist, sponsor, support group).

Chapter VII: How to Get Your Boundaries Communicated:

Best Practices for Presenting a Request

Once you've decided what you want to request of your partner, you need to identify the most skillful way of doing so. Remember—your intention is to express your needs and wants, and to create an agreement. You're not trying to control, manipulate, prove something, or be right.

You will maximize the likelihood of being heard, and possible getting an agreement, by following some simple dos and don'ts.

Do:

- Choose a time when the two of you are relatively calms and there are minimal distractions.
- Notice any physiological signs (such as rapid heart rate, sweaty palms, flushed/red skin) indicating that you may not be calm enough to have a productive conversation.
- Ask your partner if she's available to talk about something important.
- Be willing to take no for an answer and schedule another time to talk if your partner isn't available to talk when you ask her. Note: if she delays talking repeatedly, you may need to find another way of communication. For

example, leave a notepad on the kitchen counter or in her car with your requests in writing.

- Use relational questions such as
    - "I would like _____. Would you be willing to do that?"
    - "What I would like is _____. Is that something you're willing to do?"
    - "Would you be willing to _____?"

Don't:

Present your request when you're feeling highly activated/triggered. Activation is a physical and emotional experience of feeling tense, edgy, or charged up in a (non)-sexual way. Feeling activated can range in intensity from very mild to severe. Use the strategies described in the "How to Calm down Your Nervous System" to decrease your activation.

Present your request when you feel you must talk about the topic *now* and can't take no for an answer.

Persist in talking when she says she's not in a very good frame of mind to have a conversation.

Insist on getting an answer immediately when your partner wants some time to think it over.

Finally, it can be helpful to ask yourself how much the particular request you're making matters to you. The more important the issue is to you, the more attached you will be to the outcome. I often ask clients to rate issues on a scale of one to ten, ten being the highest, most important, or powerful. You can use this ten-point scale to determine how important a request is to you. This simple rating question can be helpful in clarifying your thoughts and understanding your level of investment in an outcome. I also recommend this rating tool to help you decide how to respond when your partner violates your requests.

If you rate the issue higher than a six, your attachment to the outcome is strong. In this case it is helpful to be mindful of your attachment, and to consider sharing this with your partner. For example, you can say, "I am very attached to the outcome of this request. I really want you to do what I'm asking you to do. However, I know you have a right to say yes, no, or negotiate, and that I don't have a right to get everything I want."

Successful Behaviors Self-leadership: How to Respond Assertively and Empathetically:

Communication can be extremely difficult. Even while it may feel that she "owes" you due to the betrayal, keep in mind that communication is a two-way street. When you share your requests, try to actively listen to her response. Take turns sharing and responding.

You as The Listening Person:

1. Keep in mind that *her* response is driven by *her* current degree of health, insight, and ability to communicate. In contrast, what *you* hear reflects *your* reality about the situation.

2. Consider reflecting within yourself what *your* reality looks like. ("E.g., when you tell me ... I make up that ...").

3. To increase your listening ability, position your body so that you are facing your partner. Look at your partner. Watch her expressions, feelings, and body language, and listen carefully to her words.

4. Thank the sharing person for sharing and respond:

A. Respond with needing time:

If you need time to decide how to handle her response, let the person know the time you will get back to them, e.g., "Thank you for sharing. Let me think about what you are willing to do. I will get back to you."

B. Respond with proposing an alternative to the request:

"Thank you for your response to my request.... If I hear you correctly you would like ..... *Nevertheless,* we will need to..... How does that sound?"

C. Respond with meeting her half ways:

"Thank you for sharing about ... If I hear you correctly you would like ... <u>At the same time</u>, we will need to .... You let me know that this works for you".

Postface

You may have read through the previous chapters and said "My girlfriend is nowhere near ready to respond if I were to make the above requests." Yes, choosing to repair a relationship is not for the faint of heart. At the same time, I wanted you to know what you can ask for.

Don't get me wrong: I don't want you to ask for unrealistic things. However, to make the relationship healthy (again), a baseline of mutual respect and responsiveness to healthy boundaries is a must. Use the previous chapters to become clear of what needs to be put in place for your relationship to become the healthiest it can be.

I have written this book to provide some guidance to the man who is navigating the difficult waters of betrayal. I am not saying that you will need to give the relationship another chance. At the same time, I would like you to have all the tools in place so that you can put in place what it takes for your personal life and your relationship to be sustainably healthy.

In my years working with individuals and couples trying to heal from infidelity and addiction, certain behaviors on the part of the partner can be as impactful for the success or failure of a relationship post-affair than behaviors of recovery are on the part of the betraying one.

My experience is that your personal restoration, while difficult, is possible as you are applying the chapters of this book to your situation. At the same time, your situation is complex. You are dealing with many moving parts, uncontrollable variables, and not-yet determined outcomes. My hope is that you feel inspired to reach out to others who can support- you are worth it!

With encouragement,

Sibylle Georgianna, Ph.D.

A (Non-exhaustive) Professional Resource List

Excerpt From: Sibylle Georgianna. "What Just Happened Discovering An Affair and Betrayal." iBooks.

The Association of Partners of Sex Addicts Trauma Specialists:

-For partners and family members of individuals with sex/love addiction/compulsivity.

- Offers a directory of therapists, counselors and coaches trained in Betrayal Trauma.

T (513) 847-2342

8859 Cincinnati Dayton Rd #203, West Chester Township, OH 45069

apsats.org

COSA NSO:

-For partners and family members of individuals with sex/love addiction/compulsivity.

T (763) 537-6904

PO Box 14537 Minneapolis, MN 55414

cosa-recovery.org | newhopeserenity@yahoo.com

International Institute for Trauma & Addiction Specialists:

-For individuals with sex addiction/compulsivity, partners, and family members.

T (866) 575-6853

IITAP.com

Sex and Love Addicts Anonymous

-For individuals with sex addiction/compulsivity.

T (781) 255-8825 or (781) 244-9190

PO Box 338 Norwood, MA 02062

slaafws.org | info@slaafws.org

Sex Addicts Anonymous:

-For individuals with sex addiction/compulsivity.

T (713) 869-4902 or (800) 477-8191

PO Box 70949 Houston, TX 77270

sexaa.org | info@saa-recovery.org

Sexaholics Anonymous:

-For individuals with sex addiction/compulsivity.

T (615) 370-6072 or (866) 424-8777

PO Box 3565 Brentwood, TN 37024

sa.org | saico@sa.org

Bibliography

American Psychiatric Association (2013). Diagnostic and Statistical Manual of Mental Disorders (5th ed.). Arlington, VA: American Psychiatric Publishing.

Macdonald, L.J. (2010). How to help your spouse heal from your affair: a compact manual for the unfaithful. Gig Harbor, WA: Healing Counsel Press.

Minwalla, O. (2012, July, 23). Partners of Sex Addicts Need Treatment for Trauma. The National Psychologist. Retrieved from http://nationalpsychologist.com/2012/07/partner-of-sex-addicts-need-treatment-for-trauma

Minwalla, O. (2012, September, 12). The "Co-Sex Addict" Paradigm: A Model of Diagnostic Mislabeling that Perpetuates Gender-Based Violence and the Oppression of Women. Presented at The National Conference for The Society for the Advancement of Sexual Health (SASH) (APA Accredited Presentation), San Antonio, Texas.

Scaer, R. (2012). 8 Keys to Brain-Body Balance. Take-charge strategies to heal your body and brain from stress and trauma. Norton Professional Books.

Steffens, B. A., & Means, M. (2009). Your Sexually Addicted Spouse: How Partners Can Cope and Heal.

Steffens, B. A., & Rennie, R. L. (2006). The traumatic nature of disclosure for wives of sex addicts. Sexual Addiction and Compulsivity, (13) 247-267.

Substance Abuse and Mental Health Services Administration. Impact of the DSM-IV to DSM-5 Changes on the National Survey on Drug Use and Health [Internet]. Rockville (MD): Substance Abuse and Mental Health Services Administration (US); 2016 Jun. Table 3.30, DSM-IV to DSM-5 Acute Stress Disorder Comparison. Available from:

https://www.ncbi.nlm.nih.gov/books/NBK519704/table/ch3.t30/

Sibylle Georgianna, Ph.D., EMDR-C, CST, CSAT, CMAT, CCPS is a Clinical Psychologist in Laguna Hills, California. She specializes in helping individuals and couples recovering from complex trauma, including the trauma of infidelity and compulsivity. More information can be found on her websites:

https://www.theleadershippractice.biz/

https://sexualhealthoc.com/

http://www.toolsforvitality.com/

If you have been injured by a significant other's betrayal, use the tools described in this book to identify what's going on, reduce your overwhelm, and set a clear vision.

Pick up this manual to find out what options you have, how to handle your triggers, and what you can request for you to move forward.

Sibylle Georgianna, Ph.D., EMDR-C, CST, CSAT, CMAT, CCPS is a Clinical Psychologist in Laguna Hills, California. She specializes in helping individuals and couples recovering from complex trauma, including the trauma of infidelity and compulsivity. More information:

https://www.theleadershippractice.biz/
https://sexualhealthoc.com/
http://www.toolsforvitality.com/

www.ingramcontent.com/pod-product-compliance
Lightning Source LLC
LaVergne TN
LVHW072023060526
838200LV00058B/4654